Financial Awakening

Andrés de Zamacona Garza

First Edition: August 2015

Web: www.savingslake.com

Contact: andres@savingslake.com

ISBN-13: 978-1515256434

ISBN-10: 151525643X

The worst business is a good business poorly managed.

To my wife Teresa,

who believed in me when I was just

a diamond in the rough.

(maybe I still am)

To those around me,

who through good or bad experiences forged

the person I have become.

Table of Contents

Introduction

Picture yourself in the driver's seat of one of the first working combustion-engine cars ever invented in the late 1800s. You're thrilled to do this for the first time in your life. You get comfortable on the leather chair, and grab on the tiller (used to steer before steering wheels came to exist). You spot a friend a couple of blocks away from home, and you stop your car beside him. "Howdy," you greet him and show him your brand new car. "How fast does it go?" he asks you. You look for a speedometer, but you don't find one. "Pretty fast." you answer and shrug. "How do you know when to refuel the tank?" he asks again. You look for the fuel gauge, but can't find it. You tap on the fuel tank twice, and you hear the gas moving around inside. "When this tank sounds empty."

As you can see, there was no easy way to knowing for sure at that time. Even nowadays, we don't completely trust the fuel gauge because it seems to empty faster on the last half than on the first. Still, these controls do wonders in our everyday lives. We can do a standard checkup before going out of town to know that everything is in order. We can see the speed we are going to keep a safe distance from the car in front of us in case we have to hit the brakes.

These sorts of indicators help us drive safely; maybe not without issues, but with far fewer on the whole.

We can translate this kind of thinking/indicators to our personal financial world. I cannot presume other personal finance books do not have valuable information; they sure must have, but in my opinion, they tend to be more words than facts. They focus on a psychological approach rather than a mathematical/logical one. Being wealthy financially is not only a matter of wanting; it is about knowing, planning and doing.

Throughout this book, I will give you several indicators that will help you know where you are, how fast you're going, and how fast you need to go to get where you want to be. I cannot say if it's possible for you to get where you want to be (everything has its limits and it is very important to know them), but it's of great help knowing right now if you are doing the right thing to get there.

I will also tell you some of the mistakes that people tend to make in their financial life that affect their future unknowingly. In school, we're taught to work hard, to do our homework, to get a job and to be successful in life, but sometimes one of the most important things is left out of the equation. How do we multiply our success (so that we don't have to work as much)?

Open your eyes. This is your awakening.

Chapter 1: Basics of Savings

Saving money is like putting water in a lake. You can deposit all your paychecks without touching any, and still a certain percentage of it will evaporate even on a cloudy day. It doesn't mean that you're spending it; it means every day it is worth less. You can water fewer crops with it, feed fewer animals, keep less for your living needs, etc.

Inflation affects your savings directly, so if you want to have a real measurement of what you have (wealth), you have to consider it. If you compare the inflation rates between the USA, Mexico and Europe over the past 15 years (Jan 1999- December 2014) independently, you will get that 1 USD in 1999 is equivalent to 1.46 USD in 2014. 1 EURO in 1999 is equivalent to 1.38 EURO in 2014, and 1 PESO in 1999 is equivalent to 2.15 PESOS in 2014.

Obviously, these are historical numbers and they don't predict the future like some of us would want them to, but they can help us get a good picture of what we can expect based on where we live. If I live in Mexico, and I am going to make an investment, I need a higher growth than one I would need if I were living in the US.

If you add up everything you have at point zero, which is 1999, and you don't have 2.15 times that in your Savings Lake in 2014 (if you live in Mexico), you actually lost money. You can buy less than you could at your starting point. Some things go up/down in value in time, so you have to take the "at that moment" price of what you have when adding up, rather than the price you paid for it.

Therefore, going back to the lake example, you need to consider the amount of evaporation you will experience in your lake dependent upon your location, so that you can calculate the amount of water you have to put in every year in order to keep the same level. You will also need to take into account the water you use for livestock, crops, etc. (living) so you're not taking out more than what you're putting in. Your goal is simple: make your lake grow larger, but most importantly to be a wealthy person, make a system that if you stop/lower your "work/job" water flow, it will still keep growing; or at least stay at the same level.

It's very common (and sad) to see people who made quite a bit of money during their "working days" find themselves poor during their retirement just because they didn't plan correctly. Remember that saving isn't only about having your money in the bank or under your mattress; it's about your money maintaining or increasing its value through time.

Example: Two brothers graduate from college and start working. They both are offered the same salary by different companies. Both decide to save 10% of that salary. One decides to deposit his money in the bank under a 2% interest growth, while the other decides to buy a house from his father. He is given the opportunity to buy it with an interest rate equal to inflation (4%). Which one will end with more money in fifteen years?

Taking into account that the inflation rate is 4% and the interest rate offered is 2%, the first brother will be losing around 2% each year. He will have to multiply his savings at the end of the year for the following factor:

$$Factor = \frac{(1 + 2\%)}{(1 + 4\%)} = 0.9807$$

This means that the money the first brother saved on the first year would be around 74.73% of the value that it had at the beginning (after 15 years). The money he saved on the second year would be around 76.20% of what it was worth when he deposited it and so on.

The second brother would have saved his money on something that increased its value equal to inflation (which tends to be true with houses). Because of this, his factor would be of 1.

$$Factor = \frac{(1 + 4\%)}{(1 + 4\%)} = 1.00$$

This means that what he saved on the first year is still 100% on the 15th year and so forth. Obviously this is an ideal case. If his father had charged him interest rates higher than inflation, it would have been possible for this to be the other way around.

Nevertheless, in both cases, their money is not really increasing its value through time. If you had a third person whose savings grew above inflation even if it was 1% (in which this other person would have a factor above 1) there would be a significant gap between each other after 15 years.

Let's say that these three people saved 100 USD in their different ways and waited 15 years. The first brother would have money worth 74.73 USD of present time, the second brother would still have 100 USD worth of today's money, while the third person would have 116 USD of today's money. If you divide all their final amounts by the first brother's present time money, the second brother would have around 34% more money than the first, and the third person would have 55% more money than the first brother, with just a small difference in growth but over a large amount of time.

If you take into consideration that most of the world's population has a savings growth below inflation (due to educational, cultural or political reasons) and just a few have savings growth above inflation, you'll end up with a scenario of economic inequality that gets larger each year.

For example: A businessperson invested 100 USD on his/her company with a 14% growth every year, while a second person invested 100 USD in a bank that gave him a 2% growth. The inflation rate is 4% per year. What would be their difference in a 10-year period?

$$Factor\ of\ Business\ person = \frac{(1 + 14\%)}{(1 + 4\%)} = 1.096$$

$$Factor\ of\ second\ person = \frac{(1 + 2\%)}{(1 + 4\%)} = 0.9807$$

$$Money\ after\ 10\ years\ for\ the\ business\ man$$
$$= 100\ x\ 1.096^{10} = 100\ x\ 2.5$$
$$= 250\ USD$$

$$Money\ after\ 10\ years\ for\ the\ second\ person$$
$$= 100\ x\ 0.9807^{10} = 100\ x\ 0.8229$$
$$= 82.29\ USD$$

The businessperson would have 3 times more money than the second man would. If you waited another ten years, the businessperson would have 9 times more, and if you waited another ten years after that, there would be a difference of 28 times.

Chapter 2: Expectations

You open your eyes and find yourself in the back of a movie theater. You grab a handful of butter-flavored popcorn and eat it with the utmost complacency. The movie talks about a poor boy who wished to become king. He was a dreamer and doer for most part of the picture, but he soon finds himself displeased because he's only able to become baron. He had done the unthinkable, yet he was extremely unhappy.

Our expectations can either push us forward into happiness or pull us down, even if it is in fact illogical to be feeling that way. I believe people can achieve almost anything, but not by betting on chance. For every person who becomes rich in Las Vegas, thousands lose what they bet. Can I be that one in a thousand or million? Sure, it is plausible, though highly unlikely. I would rather bet on careful planning and good execution if I am trying to become rich.

Everyone has different expectations, so first you must ask yourself: What economic expectations do I have for the future? A big house, being able to travel the world, not be an economic hassle to my children, etc. You can write down the amount of money you would need to make that possible. In how many years would I need to have that amount of money?

Example: You want to have a 500,000 USD house in 30 years. Have about 250,000 USD for retirement trips and another 400,000 USD to maintain yourself for the following 20 years while having a part time job. In summary, you would need around 1,150,000 USD of today's money, which if inflation averages similar to now, will mean you will need around twice that in 30 years' money if you are in the US.

If you add all the paychecks, you would most likely get until then (considering possible raises) times a 20% savings rate and what you currently have in your "Savings Lake" and you do not reach the number, you may be underachieving. There is no need to panic. You need to measure/know to be able to do something, else you are just going with the flow.

It does not matter if you are old or young. What matters is that you make the proper adjustments to have a better outcome. We will talk later about where the 20% came from, and how to calculate your real number.

Example: You are 35 years old and you want to retire when you are 65. You currently have an annual salary of 120,000 USD. You expect it to grow around 3% each year.

You don't know much about inflation, but the present value of what you strive for is 1,150,000 USD of today's money. That means you will really need twice that in 30 years. You currently have two cars worth 15,000 USD each (owned, not leased from the bank), a 200,000 USD house you just bought, with a mortgage of 160,000 USD, and furniture worth about 10,000 USD. You have 1,000 USD in your bank account.

Your Savings Lake is currently at 81,000 USD, but that doesn't mean it will be worth the same in 30 years. Each item has a certain life span, and if you pass that lifespan (even if it is a house), it will lose its value dramatically. In this case, we will assume the house had proper maintenance, and had a capital gain similar to inflation. This would mean it doubled its value in 30 years. The cars and furniture's current value would be lost. Therefore, you would end up with a lake savings of 80,000 USD. You will notice that I did not use the real value of the house, but the amount of the house that was really yours in that time (Current value minus Debt). That is because the remaining value is considered in the 20% of your savings ratio.

Year	Salary	Sum
1 to 5	$ 637,096.30	$ 637,096.30
6 to 10	$ 738,569.22	$ 1,375,665.52
11 to 15	$ 856,204.15	$ 2,231,869.67
16 to 20	$ 992,575.27	$ 3,224,444.94
21 to 25	$ 1,150,666.78	$ 4,375,111.72
26 to 30	$ 1,333,938.17	$ 5,709,049.88

You get the 20% of your 5,709,050 USD, which is 1,141,810 USD. The total sum of your lake at year 30 would be 1,221,810 USD. This would mean you do not have as much money in your Savings Lake as you expected.

Some might read this and say, "Hey, I'm only 25-30 years old and retirement is not at the top of my mind". Well, you could actually do this exercise and just change the time where you are going to need the money.

Example: You are a young adult who graduated from university just a couple of years ago. You want to make about 100,000 USD per year of today's money in ten years. You know that people in your field usually earn only about 60,000 USD after ten years. You currently earn 30,000 USD. What can you do?

Inflation rates of 3% in ten years mean you would need about 35% more. Your goal will now be to earn 135,000 USD per year by then. Taking into account that most likely salaries will increase consistent with inflation, you would be earning around 81,000 USD in your tenth year. You still need 54,000 USD a year to meet your goal.

- Goal: 135,000 USD (100,000 USD of today's money)
- Expected salary: 81,000 USD (60,000 USD of today's money)
- Requirement: 54,000 USD extra a year by then

You can then plan how much money you can save during that time from your salary. If you plan to save 10% of your salary in your bank account during those ten years to invest on something after your tenth year, it will be as follows:

- Savings percentage: 10% of your annual salary.
- Ten year Salary: 550,000 USD
- Ten year Savings: 55,000 USD

On your tenth year, you would need to make 54,000 USD out of the 55,000 USD you saved. That means your 55,000 USD would have to grow 98% above inflation each year to maintain its value and give you the 54,000 USD extra you want. That sounds very unrealistic.

If you make your savings grow 10% above inflation each year and you keep depositing 10% of your salary each year, you will have 81,000 USD on your tenth year instead of the 55,000 USD. This means you will need 67% above inflation for that 81,000 USD, so you get the extra you want.

By knowing this, you can either adjust the amount of money you will be saving per year, look for the business you need to create an above 10% inflation growth per year or even lower your salary expectations. You now have the knowledge at hand to make a decision.

You must also remember that your expectations can affect your judgment, and potentially cause you to make poor decisions. For example, someone who wants to imitate the life of someone very wealthy might decide to spend all their money on a very expensive car. While this will bring immediate satisfaction, the reality is that cars maintain little of their value through time, so instead of actually saving money, you will be losing growth opportunity.

People who are really wealthy (not just temporarily) spend their money on valuable things in a certain span of time. If they actually spend all their money in a single year to buy everything they currently own they will give their savings a huge hit, and they could stop being wealthy. If you end up with a lot of money: don't overspend. Your material (low quality assets) growth shouldn't demolish your economic (Savings Lake) growth.

Example: You are a factory worker with an hourly wage of 20 USD. You live in a rented house, own a 6,000 USD car and having nothing in your bank account. You win the lottery and end up with a million USD! Your Savings Lake is now 1,006,000 USD (for this exercise, we're assuming a tax free winning). You go out shopping houses, cars, trips, etc. You buy a 500,000 USD house, two 100,000 USD cars, and spend 50,000 USD on trips. You triple your expenses in a year and stop working. How long will you last?

Considering that you used to spend 42,000 USD a year before winning the lottery, you would be spending around 126,000 USD a year. This means you will be out of cash by the end of the second year. Since cars lose their value at a rate of around 15% per year (percentage varies between cars), your cars will be worth around 150,000 USD. Since your house increased its value 3%, it will now be worth 515,000 USD. Your Savings Lake would be 665,000 USD by the second year. You will need to sell the cars to maintain yourself for one more year, and by the third year you would be selling the house.

If you had looked for a way to increase your Savings Lake 10% without inflation, you could have had the equivalent of a yearly paycheck from your current job forever without lowering your Savings Lake size. Where is the real problem?

Imagine you did not win the lottery, but you got the same amount of money due to working hard for a long time. If you went on a shopping rampage, you will end up having the same outcome as above. It is not about where the money is coming from, but on what you are spending your money.

Chapter 3: Time

Time is the most important non-renewable resource in our lives, but it is also one of our most important allies if used wisely. If you read 1 book every month, you will have read 12 books by the end of the year; Simple math. If someone tried to have the same knowledge as you (in books), they would need to read the 12 books, plus the books you would have read in the time they take to catch up to you. Hard? Yes. Impossible? Not really. If you had read the same amount of books per year for five years, you will have read 60 books. If someone who wasted their time tried to reach you, they would have a very difficult time doing so.

The same happens with money. At first, we're all in similar conditions. Yes, someone could be winning twice or three times as much as you, but if you would make a good business move in your first years, you could actually reach him or her and have the same amount of money (or even more). The problem lies when a lot of time goes by. I know that if wealth were a competition, we would all be losers with just one rich winner at the top, so it's not exactly like that. It is more of a personal competition, where you make the right moves to reach what you expect, and get a sense of achievement. Money is not the source of happiness, but the lack of it can indeed make people sad.

Work experience isn't based on the amount of time you have been doing something, but in the amount of knowledge you have accumulated. It is possible that someone in a year's time has more knowledge than someone who has been doing ten years the same. No one accepts that they are wrong or incomplete if they have being doing something for ten years, even if they are wrong.

Use your spare time (at home or work) to learn something new that could complement your job or investments. This could greatly influence your success in what you do. You don't need to focus entirely on that, but a couple of hours a week could mean you know more than your peers in a year. If you are an engineer, learn how to do accounting, and learn about taxes. If you are in the accounting sector, you could learn how to program to automate your work. If you work in a restaurant, you could learn how to do flowcharts to reduce time in certain processes. If you are an architect, you could learn to negotiate and increase your profit when buying materials. If you are a househusband or a housewife, you could learn management and investment techniques. Working on something specific does not prevent you from learning something outside of the area of your expertise. It is very healthy to know more of the outside. It gives you the ability to make integral decisions rather than narrow minded ones.

Each year you could specialize in something different so that in a matter of years you could be a complete professional and not just an operator of a certain tasks. There are several ways to increase your savings: you either increase your income (you can have several incomes, not only the one from your job) or decrease your expenses. By increasing your income and not increasing your expenses, you are lowering the ratio of your income needed to live.

One main difference between a wealthy person and someone not wealthy is the ratio of their expenses/savings to their income. If you are someone with a very low wage, you will use most of your money in daily needs. (Example: Transportation, Food, Education, etc.) If you are someone with a high income, very little of it will go into the basics, so you'll have a higher percentage of your income to either save or invest. If you make your money grow bigger, your ratio will go down and you will have a higher percentage to invest.

Chapter 4: Spending

You open the door to your recently purchased house in the suburbs. You and your family are extremely happy. You were saving money for quite some time, and well, everything just seemed to line up for this wonderful moment. You sit on the couch and grab your tablet to check your bank account balance. Well, it looks almost empty, but the house was worth it. You didn't go over your budget, just as you planned. Yes, you still owe part of the house, but it is an investment that will pay off in due time. Not paying rent and living where it is yours. You have a safe job, so you have nothing to worry. It's just a matter of time to accumulate more money in order to fill the house with nice accessories, and furniture. What could you be doing wrong?

It is not a matter of right and wrong: it is a matter of choice. Each dollar you spend is a dollar that's splitting up into two parts. One part is gone forever (you will never see it again) and another part goes in your Savings Lake. It all depends on what you spend. There's nothing wrong with spending on something that will all go into nothingness, like food, because we still need to fulfill our basic needs. We can still manage ourselves a bit better, though.

Example: You are buying a house for 300,000 USD. You are making a down payment of 20% and will be paying the rest at a 4% interest rest for the next 20 years. You also pay 1% of taxes for buying the house.

Without doing much math, you will get the following:

- Down payment for the house: 60,000   USD
- Taxes: 3,000   USD
- Principal (Capital payment): 240,000   USD
- Interests: 118,131   USD

After 20 years, you will have spent 421,131 USD on a house that had an initial market value of 300,000 USD. This means that if you stay the whole 20 years, 71.2% of all you paid would go on your Savings Lake, and the rest would be lost. I am not taking into consideration house capital gains in this case because I am assuming they are near equal to inflation. Therefore, even if it goes up in value 3% per year, your money would be worth 3% less because of inflation every year. Because of that, I am considering they cancel out.

If you sold the house on the tenth year, meaning you leave before you end up paying, you would have paid 252,065.87 USD and would still owe 155,617 USD. If you sold the house for the same 300,000 USD and paid the mortgage, you would get only 144,383 USD back. This means that after 10 years, only 57.2% of what you paid would have gone into your Savings Lake.

In this scenario, what's interesting is not the amount of money (because we are not considering capital gains nor inflation), but the ratio going into our Savings Lake. You get at most 70% if you keep the house the whole 20 years, and 50% or below if you stay with the house 10 years or fewer. It's not quite the best investment. We are also not considering any "maintenance" the house would require after that many years.

If you do the same exercise with cars, you will get even lower Savings Lake deposits because there is capital loss (almost all cars lose value over time) and interest lost without considering inflation. You would actually be looking at something near the 30% savings deposit.

How can we have a quick measure of the amount of deposits we are making in our lake?

Savings Lake Deposit Ratio (SLDR)

$$SLDR = \frac{\sum(Expend * C) + (Income - \sum Expend)}{Income}$$

Expend = Money used up individually

$$\Sigma\text{Expend} = \text{Total of Money used up}$$

$$C = \text{Independent Expenditure Ratio}$$

$$\text{Income} = \text{Total Money received}$$

Example: If you had an income of 3,200 USD per month and you spent 1,500 USD on your house leased for 20 years, 600 USD on your car, 800 USD on everything else, and you saved 300 USD on your bank account, you would have the following result.

$$\frac{(1500 * 0.71 + 600 * 0.3 + 800 * 0) + (3{,}200 - 1500 - 600 - 800)}{3{,}200}$$

$$\text{Saving Lake Deposit Ratio} = (1{,}245 + 300) / 3{,}200 = 0.48$$
$$\text{or } 48\%$$

This means that 48% of what you make goes into your Savings Lake without considering inflation. This will be considered in a simpler way later on.

Remember that if you spend the 300 USD that you saved later on, you will affect your Savings Lake Deposit Ratio for that particular month. For example, let's assume that you spend those 300 USD one month later in a party, added to the 300 USD you'd have normally saved.

$$\frac{(1500 * 0.71 + 600 * 0.3 + 800 * 0 + 600 * 0) + (3{,}200 - 1500 - 600 - 800 - 600)}{3{,}200}$$

Saving Lake Deposit Ratio = (1,245 - 300) / 3,200 = 0.29
or 29%

Example 2: If you had an income of 3,200 USD per month and you spent 1,500 USD on your house leased for 20 years, 600 USD on your car, 1,200 USD on everything else (you would have to put 100 USD on your cards to do this) you would have the following result:

$$\frac{(1500 * 0.71 + 600 * 0.3 + 1200 * 0) + (3{,}200 - 1500 - 600 - 1200)}{3{,}200}$$

Saving Lake Deposit Ratio = (1,245 - 100) / 3,200 = 0.35
or 35%

This means that 35% of what you make goes into your Savings Lake, but you have a future problem. If you keep this way of working, you would increase your expenditures by paying credit card interests and still owe the 100 USD. Your ratio will have a tendency to go down.

The saving lake deposit ratio is used to see a tendency in your expending, not actually know the amount going into your Savings Lake. As you may have noticed, in the first years of mortgage, you pay mostly interest, and in the later years, you pay more to principal/capital.

You will not always be able to avoid having low ratio or zero ratio expenditures, because we all have basic needs, but you can still measure yourself and know where you can make the changes. Once you have a stable ratio that allows you save money, you can now start thinking of multiplying it.

I generally do not advise to count clothing, electronics or other personal items as part of your Savings Lake (with an expenditure ratio above zero) because people generally end up giving them away or putting them in the trash. If you buy used musical instruments or other items in order to sell them, they are in fact part of your Savings Lake, and you have to treat them as such.

When you buy furniture for your house, while at first it may look like an investment, it may not be one. It all depends on their resale value. There are certain types of furniture (antiques) that hold their value through time (or have low to moderate loses) with proper care. This type of item can be considered as part of your Savings Lake until you cannot sell them, or their market value is close to nothing.

Personal Finances Vocabulary

There are three things you can spend your money on: **Investment** (grows with time), Savings (maintains or slightly decreases its value through time) and Void (no remaining value).

When you go to a bank and are offered a growth above inflation, you are being offered an Investment. A good or bad investment depends on the amount of growth you get. Generally, banks will offer low growth investments because they have to make money too out of your money. They also tend to have low or no risk at all. There are other investments that could obviously have a higher payout but also a higher risk. Risk does not mean failure and it is not a gamble. There are certain projects that have high payouts and low risks. It all depends what you are doing.

If you go to the bank and are offered a growth below inflation, you are being offered a savings options. Savings is when you get less or equal for what you have. Putting your money in a non-growing bank account in the US means it will be worth around 97% after the first year and 94% after the second one. Each year less.

Just like specified above, you can save a percentage of the amount of money you are spending. This is still considered savings, because it will accumulate in your Savings Lake. Obviously, someone who is investing their money will make their Savings Lake get bigger much faster than someone who is just spending.

Void is just spending that has no remaining value. You ate your hamburger, it tasted really good, but that is all you are getting for you money (besides perhaps a couple ounces of fat). That's about it.

Void and savings are interlaced, while investment is in another "more refined" category.

Chapter 5: Savings Lake

You take a deep breath in front of your half mile radius lake. On the other side of where you are, you can see your livestock closing in to refresh themselves after a hot day. You open your eyes wide and see something that you had never seen before. A large chunk of ice lies in the center of the lake with its tip just barely above the surface. It could actually be an iceberg! Most of its volume lies below the water, so there is probably quite a bit you cannot see. It's curious how the sun is not melting the ice, but who cares right? It is still water in the lake.

We already learned that buying houses and cars are not precisely good investments like we were taught to think, but they are in fact ways to save money (even if they are bad ways to save it). If you buy a house without mortgage, it would have a tendency to stay the same value across time (with tax and maintenance loses), while if you buy a car, it would surely lose its value no matter what. Nevertheless, they are actually putting water into your Savings Lake, but they are not liquid savings. They are captive savings, similar to the ice in your lake. You can't really use them to invest in something else, or for livestock use.

I will separate the lake into three parts: Liquid savings (Money), Captive Savings (Assets) and Savings Oil (Debt). While they all seem to add to the volume of the lake, oil is actually negating the effect of the others and it can pollute your savings ratio.

$$Savings\ Lake = Liquid\ Savs\ (\$) + Captive\ Savs\ (Assets) - Savings\ Oil\ (Debt)$$

Example: If you have 10,000 USD saved in the bank, a house worth 300,000 USD and a debt of 250,000 USD. How big is your Savings Lake?

$$Savings\ Lake = 10,000\ USD + 300,000\ USD - 250,000\ USD$$

Your Savings Lake total would be 60,000 USD.

Buying things with debt will increase your future expenditure because of interest rates, so it will decrease your savings ratio. Therefore, while it may seem like your Savings Lake got bigger first, you are actually making it grow slower (or even decrease) in the long run. The only way to get around it is to invest debt, and that the investment actually pays the debt and the interests while giving you a margin.

This is the correct way to measure the size of your Savings Lake. From there, you can compare between years (and use an inflation correction formula) to see if your lake actually grew or if you lost money.

Savings Grow Rate

$$= \frac{\dfrac{Savings\ Lake\ 2014}{(1 + Inflation\ between\ 2014\ and\ 2013)} - Savings\ Lake\ 2013}{Savings\ Lake\ 2013}$$

Example: If your Savings Lake size in 2013 was 60,000 USD, the size of your lake on 2014 is 63,000 USD, and the inflation rate on the US from 2013 to 2014 is 1.6%. What is your real savings Grow Rate?

$$Savings\ Grow\ Rate = \frac{\dfrac{63,000}{(1 + 1.6/100)} - 60,000}{60,000}$$
$$= 0.033\ or\ 3.3\ \%$$

In one of the following chapters, you will learn the pros and cons of investing debt, and how you can make a business out of thin air. This is especially true if you live in countries with low interest rates.

If you live in a country with high inflation rates, it's advisable to either keep your money invested in something that keeps/increases their value through time, or move it out to another currency where it won't lose value. If you live in Mexico or elsewhere, you can have a

USD bank account; there is no need to move to another country. If you are unsure of exchange rates, you can go to a bank and try to buy an exchange rate forward. This type of instruments will ensure your exchange rate with a marginal loss.

For example: You live in a country where the inflation between 2014 and 2015 is 6%. You had 60,000 currency last year and you have 63,000 currency this year. Did you grow that year?

$$Savings\ Grow\ Rate = \frac{\frac{63{,}000}{(1 + 6/100)} - 60{,}000}{60{,}000}$$
$$= -0.01\ or\ -1.0\ \%$$

You lost money even if your bank account says otherwise. If time went by, you would be able to buy each year less and less. If you continue this course, your Savings Lake would be worth 90% in 10 years of what it currently is. Small amount of losses add to big losses over a long period of time.

Inflation creates havoc in your savings if you leave them unattended. Every quarter of a year, check the national bank estimations so that you are aware that everything is going according to plan. If you are expecting high inflation and there is no way for you to get a project that will give you equal or above inflation growth, it may be time to buy some assets that will maintain their value.

Just as inflation can destroy your savings, growth per year can really make a difference in the end. If you had a growth of 5% above inflation on your Savings Lake per year, after 10 years you would have 62% more money. If you kept that same growth for ten more years, you would have 165% more than what you had at first. This doesn't seem like much, but it does make a difference in your life.

How often should you do a Savings Lake check-up? You should probably do this once or twice per year, once per year being the minimum. If you do it every six months, you will be able to catch certain tendencies to make adjustments, but it really depends on what you are doing. People with long-term investments should check once a year, while people with companies or short-term should check every quarter.

Chapter 6: Multiplication

Investment return is like the Earthquake's Richter scale (it is a logarithmic scale) in which each time it goes up the scale, it's ten times stronger but with a base of 2. What it means is that each time it doubles, it takes the same amount of time to double again (in theory). Imagine inflation was so high you would need to double the amount of money every ten years to have an equal living cost. After the 30 years, you would need to double three times: 1 USD would be 8 USD. The inflation rate in this scenario would be 7.2% per year. Doesn't sound like that much, right? If you had a growth of 7.2% more than your country's inflation rate, you would end up having 8 times more in 30 years. Obviously, with small amounts of money it's very simple to achieve that, because you're not really affecting the market. With high amounts of money, your growth tends to be a tad smaller in percentage because you start having market or operational limitations. When your company is so big that you can't control it, maybe it is time to change to investing in the stock market.

Investments such as houses offer low growth rate even if you rent it. As I stated before, the capital growth of a house tends to be similar to inflation (average, some go down and some go up), but the rent you charge is what gives you that extra growth. If you charge 5% of the house value per year for renting, you will have enough money to buy another house in around 15 years (minus maintenance) while keeping the same value of your initial "deposit". If you rented both houses now, you would have four houses in another 15 years and eight houses in 30 years. This means that if you start renting houses when you are 30 years old, you could have 8 rental houses at the age of 75 as a retirement fund. A fund that gives you around 40% of a house worth each year while maintaining its value through time (and inflation).

Obviously, 45 years is a lot of time, and many things could happen in those years, but it is a plausible way to make it work. The problem with this method is that we are mentally inclined to want immediate gratification. We don't want to wait 45 years to get something back, even if it was the best choice we could ever make. Most people would use the money they get from the first rented house to increase their living expenses and so, prevent growth and reinvestment.

The top problem of an investor is desire for immediate payback, and the only thing that gives you immediate payback is a job. You work for a week and you are paid at the end of it. So what can you do? You actually have a couple of successful choices.

We talked about expectations in one of our earlier chapters and we made a table of our future job incomes. This table can help us know how much money we are going to receive and the healthy saving ratio habits we require to make enough money to invest. How much money do you need? It depends on how much money you want to make in a certain period.

Example: You want to have enough money to start a business that costs 250,000 USD to start. You currently have about 10,000 USD in cash. Your total income is 200,000 USD per year. If you saved 10% per year (and put it on a bank account that gives you something equal to inflation each year) you would need 12 years. You could actually make semi businesses that would lead you were you want in less time.

After the first year, you would have approximately 30,000 USD, just enough to either: Buy cars to resell and make a margin for each sale, or buy things from China/etc. and sell them throughout the year on the internet or to people you know. Things that will not require your full attention (meaning you will not leave work), but can help you multiply your money. Do not go high on inventory; your objective is not to become wealthy from one day to another (or poor if nothing sells). It is to create a safe path to your bigger goal. These small sales can offer you higher growth rates without necessarily tapping the market limitations.

For example: You buy a food/coke machine that is worth 5,000 USD. You also invest 500 USD in product inventory and expect to have a margin of 50% of what you sale. This means you'll sell that 500 USD of products at 1,000 USD. You also expect to sell the 100% of the products each month (you will restock the inventory every week so that it never runs low).

It didn't go as expected, and instead of having a profit of 500 USD monthly you get a profit of 300 USD. If you divide the 5,500 USD by 300 USD/Month you will get a return in about 18 months. You reinvest everything you got back in another coke machine and now you are getting 600 USD monthly. You now take 9 months to be able to buy another coke machine. Once you buy the third coke machine you are getting 900 USD a month, and after 6 months you are able to buy a fourth machine.

Let's say that the life of a coke machine is 5 years. When you actually have to get rid of the first machine, you'll have around 13 machines that still have a lifespan between 18 and 60 months. You will be able to buy a new machine every month when you have 18 machines, which will be before you have to get rid of the second. This kind of multiplication process can apply to any kind of business that has easy replication. The most important thing is not to continue down that road if you tap the market limit. If you do, you'll have to change your business to something else that has a higher value and doesn't tap that market. For example, you start with coke machines, then move to car rentals, then move to heavy machinery, then move to houses, etc.

The higher the growth rate, the faster it will multiply. Things with small value tend to multiply faster than things with higher value.

You can always search for ways to invest debt, which could be great if you keep them at a safe level. You will read in the next chapter how debt can increase your growth rate.

Chapter 7: Investing Debt

A magician bows before you. He holds a black iconic hat with a white ribbon around its base. He shows you the inside of the hat and even lets you search for any hidden chambers. Everything looks legit. He then puts on the hat and waves his long black wooden wand. He gives it a slight tap. He then removes it and you cannot believe it! A rabbit hops happily on top of his head.

Debt can be both a curse and a blessing, but it isn't magic, though sometimes it can seem to be. There are really two kinds of debt: those used to buy things that will lower their value (and hence debt will increase your expenses) and those used to buy assets that will raise their value more than the interests they charge (and hence increase your income).

For no logical reason, people tend to accept the first one and fear the second one when it should be the other way around. If you go buy a car with debt, you are "investing", and when you go start a business with debt, you are buying "risk". Yes, buying something that will only bring you pleasure and no profit is a sure bet: a lost one. The right way to debt investment is to do it in a moderate level, just like if you were buying a car.

Example: You have a 2,000 USD monthly salary and you use only 1,500 for your living expenses. You wish to earn more money, but you are not saving enough money to start a business. You are sure that if you bought a used car for 15,000 USD, cleaned it up a bit yourself and spend less than 100 USD, you could sell it in 16,500 USD in a month or two.

You go to the bank and ask for money to buy the car. They give you a 4% annual rate on a 48-month loan with no charge on early payments. You have monthly payments of 350 USD for which only 50 USD are interests. You take six months to sell it. Your total income is 16,500 USD and your expenses are 15,400 USD. You earn 1,100 USD by investing 350 USD monthly in a six-month period. It is not the business opportunity of the lifetime (this example), but it works.

- Buy car at 15,000 USD with a loan
- Spend 100 USD to clean car
- You pay 50 USD of interest each month
- You pay 300 USD of capital each month
- You sell the car for 16,500 USD after six months

Profit = 16,500 USD (Sold at) – 15,000 USD (Bought at) – 50 USD x 6 months (Interest Rate) – 100 USD (Cleaning) = 1,100 USD

You don't subtract the capital payment because this goes directly to pay the loan. This affects you, however, because you are investing money while you sell the car.

Month	Loan	Interest Paid	Money Invested
0	15,000 USD	0 USD	0 USD
1	14,700 USD	50 USD	350 USD
2	14,400 USD	100 USD	700 USD
3	14,100 USD	150 USD	1,050 USD
4	13,800 USD	200 USD	1,400 USD
5	13,500 USD	250 USD	1,750 USD
6	13, 200 USD	300 USD	2,100 USD

Example: You want to build a house to sell it, but you only have half of what is needed to buy the land and do the construction (whole construction and land is 400,000 USD and selling at 460,000 USD). You know that the margin of selling a house is of 15%. If you asked for a loan to pay the half of what you do not have at an 8% interest rate, you'd be paying 16,000 USD in interest annually. This means that if in a year you do the whole construction and made the sale, your numbers would look like this:

House sold at:	460,000	USD
Your investment:	200,000	USD
Bank loan:	200,000	USD
Interests:	16,000*	USD
Profit:	44,000	USD

*If you asked for the loan at the beginning, and not half way through the construction

Your profit ratio over your investment would be 22% instead of the 15% you would get if you had not asked for a loan. If it takes longer to sell the house than what you want, you can always drop the price a bit to try to sell it faster. Remember that profit over investment should be calculated per year and not per event. If you have a 50% profit return in 10 years, it means you had roughly a 4.2% growth per year, which is not that good. The opposite happens if you have things with a low event profit but many repetitions per year. They end up adding up to a good interest rate.

Just like what happened when you bought the car to sell it, you need to take into consideration the amount of money you have to pay for the loan so that you can actually keep paying it. If you cannot pay then they will charge you with extra interest rates.

Chapter 8: Baggage

"Change your life forever! Just stop eating, sending your kids to school, have a place to sleep and you'll be rich!"

Perhaps what you have read until now sounds wonderful, but you look at your current situation and it does not look positive/plausible. You already have kids to feed, bills to pay and just too much baggage. My best recommendation is not to panic. If you do a Savings Lake Size Checkup, and you find out you are on the negative side or with a negative tendency, you can start planning a way to get out of your problems. It will not be easy, but it is better than doing nothing.

If you have a lot of debt, your first step should be restructuring it. Try to free up all the high interest rate credits and move them to lower interest rate ones with a longer term. The goal of this is try avoiding having a negative savings rate because that will surely lead you to failure. If you have a growing debt, you must focus on not letting it grow more. A bigger debt means more problems, which is exactly what you don't want.

Example: You have 5,000 USD in each credit card (you have two) with an interest rate of 15% each. That means you're generating 1,500 USD in interest per year. If you are capable of only paying the interest rate, you will never get rid of the debt. It is advisable to restructure your debt into a single bank loan. You may even get a bank loan with almost half the interest rate of a credit card. You would be paying exactly the same amount of money, but the interests generated per year would be around 800 USD instead of 1,500 USD. That means you are paying to principal/capital 700 USD per year. The interests generated will go down each year and your principal payment will go up. Eventually you will finish paying your whole debt. Get rid of your credit cards while you do this because you might be tempted to get a bigger debt.

The whole concept of the Savings Lake is for you to see your possessions as money, and not give them a sentimental value. This does not mean you don't appreciate what you have; it means you can get rid of it if that would get you closer to your goal. If you have a property that would avoid your debt getting to unsustainable levels, I would suggest you sell it. I would suggest the same if you had a property that if you sold you could make more money doing something else with it. It is not about doing what feels right; it is about doing what *is* right.

It is not always like this, but getting baggage is about making a decision. Good or bad, it is a decision that will have certain repercussions. If you have kids, your expenses will rise. That does not mean having kids is wrong; it could be a perfect life decision, but it is the effect of having kids. It is the same when buying a house, buying a car, going on vacations, etc.

A Positive economic analysis focuses on the facts and cause-and-effects of certain decisions or phenomena. It is used to see the "what is" and not the "what ought to be". What is the inflation of the US? 3.6%. The answer is always 3.6% even if that is a good thing or a bad thing. These control numbers help the government change their economic strategies to raise or lower the inflation. You should do the same with your economic numbers.

Analyze the amount of money your baggage will need in the future so you can plan for it. If you know your kids will need to go to college in a couple of years, you need to take it into account. Otherwise, you could believe that you are actually saving and growing when the money you saved is already tied to a future expenditure.

Chapter 9: Liquid vs Captive Savings and Debt

She was rich; just plain rich. She had hundreds of acres of land, and a house that was just outstanding. Her Savings Lake was as big as it gets. She even left her job a couple of years ago to see her wealth get bigger without much work, but there was something that kept her uneasy. Every day she opened her window to see her lake, and she knew something was wrong. Yes, there was no debt at all, but there was almost no liquid water. Almost all of it was a huge chunk of ice that was getting bigger and bigger. One day, the taxman came to visit her to charge her just a small percent of her earnings that year, but she had no money to pay him. Selling land was not something that could be done in a matter of days. She was in a bit of a bind.

Every company and person requires money (cash) to survive. We cannot survive with only our assets (unless we sell them), even if they are growing in value. It is not just a matter of making your Savings Lake as big as you can; you have to do it in a sustainable way.

You can use liquid savings (money) at any given moment to buy anything you want, be it something that has a high savings ratio (above 1) or a low one. Its main con is that it does not produce more money by itself. Yes, you can buy assets such as government bonds from a bank that can ensure you can withdraw your money (sell the asset) whenever you want, but they are still assets. A company that buys electric material to resell is actually turning their liquid savings (or debt) into assets expecting to receive a higher return. Money does not produce money by itself if it is not being invested.

Captive savings on the other hand vary from those that are short-term, long-term and everything in-between. Generally, short-term ones (like the interests offered by the bank) have low interest payouts. They practically pay you less than inflation, but they represent a safety net that you can count on. How big of a safety net do you require? It depends on your other captive savings, expenditures, and debt.

Example: You bought a new car a week ago without waiting to sell your old one. Your new car requires you to pay 500 USD a month. You plan to pay your new debt with the old car but you haven't found a buyer. Your salary is 4,000 USD a month and you require 3,600 USD to live. You have 1000 USD in your bank account.

Each month you have a deficit of 100 USD that will eat your bank account slowly. Even if your Savings Lake is actually getting bigger, if you do not handle the problem in time you will become unsustainable and end up having to ask for a loan to pay another loan. You will then increase your expenditures with bank interest that will eat your savings.

There is no correct mix between liquid savings and captive savings; you have to calculate it. The example above could be several integers more, and it would be the same outcome. My advice is to avoid those kind of deficits when investing in any asset. I prefer to have a growing liquid savings every month, and when I have enough of them, I convert them to middle to long-term assets. Try to keep most of your liquid savings in bank investments when you don't have them invested in anything. Bank investments are not real investments. They are only helpful when you're waiting and do not want to lose as much money to inflation.

Chapter 10: Credit Cards

You are a great businessperson. People know you because you have the best ideas in town, are hard worker, and they know someday you will be unstoppable. You are on the line for a loan interview with the bank. This is the only thing that stands before your obvious success as an entrepreneur. Right behind you is another person in line; a fellow student you knew once in high school who was not so bright. The manager of the bank comes your way and asks you politely to enter her office. You step right inside and sit down where she tells you, "Good day. I hear you want a loan for a very important business." You nod and smile. "I have checked the records and you've never had any credits with us or any bank. Is that true?" You nod again and respond, "That wouldn't be a problem, right? I am a hard worker and have a lot of academic and work recommendations." She looks at you and sighs, "Unfortunately, our bank's policy is to never give this type of loan to people who do not have a credit background. Once you have credit background of a couple of years, you can come right back. Thank you." You leave the room obviously displeased, and find your old acquaintance singing her loan papers.

A credit background is necessary if you want to get a loan, good or bad. As stated before, debt can increase either your expenses or your income. It depends on how you use it and for what you use it. It's important for young people to have a low limited credit card in order to train themselves; not to learn to pay interests when buying non-saving items (though paying interest would likely raise your credit score if you keep paying it), but to be responsible with debt and have a credit background. Always paying the total of your credit card might be a bad thing for the bank (though they still get commissions from the companies that did the sale), but it is still a good background. If a young person gets a credit card in their early years, they will have a credit background by the time they start working. At this time (as a parent), you could also see trends in their spending and make the proper corrections.

Example: You get a credit card for you daughter with a max debt of 500 USD. You give her an allowance of 100 USD per week (which includes gasoline and personal items). You deposit her allowance into a bank account from which she has to pay the credit card (online).

You will be able to see trends in her spending. She could be the totalitarian type in which each time she uses it she pays it right away. She could also be the type that waits for the payment date and pays it completely. The worst that could happen is that she is that type that does not manage herself, and she overspends her next allowance before she receives it. You can check where and how she spends her money, and if any of the things she buys has a residual value that goes into her "Savings Lake".

Credit cards are excellent to teach lessons if used wisely. In this example, it was about a month's pay, the limit of the credit card. If she screws up it is a lesson where the repercussions could last a month or two. If you give her even more of a credit in the start, she could actually hurt your finances and the lesson learned would be a different one from the one you want. You would probably learn not to trust your kids with money, which is wrong.

You must also remember that credit cards tend to have the highest interest rates in the market, so you must avoid using them as credit. Use them as a way to avoid having money in your wallet/purse, and as a way to improve your credit background for real investments you want to make for your businesses. Without increasing your expenditures, you can gain points that you could later use to get gifts.

Chapter 11: Stages of life

While each of us make different choices in our lifetimes which affect our present and future economic wellbeing, we all go through several common life stages. We can decide not to go through one (such as marriage, parenthood, etc.), but they are still not uncommon for us.

Childhood

In our childhood and adolescence (0-20 year old approx.), we are in most cases dependent on our parents' economic choices. We can sometimes decide on what we spend our money, but generally any money spending will go to entertainment, basic needs or clothing (which have savings ratio of zero). We consider saving money just depositing it in the bank for future needs. There is actually no consideration of real investment.

We have little to no notion of the cost of getting money, and because of that we have no real interest in saving much.

Young adult

Once we start being more independent and start considering ourselves as single (without dependents, 21-

28 years old), we look for jobs to cover our basic needs or any personal wishes. In the Mexican middle class, young adults become independent when they finish their education (university) and get a job, though they still are somewhat economically dependent to their parents because they live with them and they pay for most (if not all) of their needs. They usually move out when they get married, or when they are 30 years old or more. If they do not have enough money to go to a university, they simply don't go, and start working right away.

In the US, young adults usually move out when they go to college. Many find themselves in situations where their income is equal or lower to their outcome (because of lack of parent financial support or bad expenditure). If their parents are not able (or do not want to) pay for their university, they are forced to get a loan that will trip their growth in years to come.

While maybe none of these scenarios apply to us, we still tend to have low savings ratio expenditures. We spend our money in living (no savings ratio), entertainment (no savings ratio), vacations (no saving ratio) and cars (low saving ratio). If we do save some of our money, we tend to just deposit it in the bank without looking for investments that can give us above inflation growth.

Marriage

We grow older and find the person (or not) we want to marry. We want to have a big celebration so we end up spending most (if not all) in the wedding. Some of us might even get in debt from the wedding because it's "once in a lifetime". At this stage, we become completely independent from our parents, and we start caring about our future. We then make the best investment we were taught to do: buy a house. We don't have kids or any other type of dependencies aside from our partner, so we spend what money we have left in either buying a car or going on constant trips. We believe we are completely hassle free and tend to have low or no savings ratio on everything else but the house and/or cars. We start getting better jobs, and we start thinking about making the next obvious step in life: having children.

Children

By this time, we have savings ratio of around a 25-30% because we are spending most of what we earn in the house or in cars. We are around 29-34 years old. We start using credit cards in our everyday lives. We start buying things with low or no savings ratio in monthly payments because it is very comfortable and we don't "feel" the expense.

Our incomes go up with time, but so do our expenses. While before, the house and car were probably around 40% or more of what we made, it goes down to around a 20-30%. The remaining money goes into living, vacations, education, and furniture. This means that our savings ratio goes down to 15-20%. More money did not mean more savings. People tend to live like this from 35-50 years old. Usage of credit cards go into moderate to high debt levels because everyone has "emergencies".

Late adulthood

At this age, we get another boost in our income because we go into a higher level in our jobs. We then go again into selling the house we had and buying a new, more expensive one. Our savings ratio goes back to the 20-30%, but just for a moment before we are again forced to reality when our kids go to college. They might need a car, right?

Once we hit around 55, we have a mind blowing realization: we are going to retire in ten years. We then gather (save) as much money as we can without investing anything because we believe it's too risky to invest when it's the last money we are going to receive. We wrongly believe that the 10% of money we saved for the last ten years will be enough to sustain our lives in retirement. We have a big house, and a couple of years' worth of income. After we finish our retirement savings, we sell the big house and move into a much smaller one to continue living.

Chapter 12: Ignorance is not bliss

You're an adventurer like no other. You roam a tropical forest in search of hidden treasures. You are equipped with a leather whip, a sharp machete, a small shovel and a map. Yes, the exact directions to a bright and wealthy future that is just up ahead. You slash some bushes with your machete to make a way through and you come upon a marvelous spectacle. There is a huge temple that smells like gold and butter is about a mile away from your current location. You are very excited, and what's best: rich. Stinking rich.

You walk slowly to the temple and find yourself in some wet soil. Not fretting, you keep going to your goal even if it is ankle deep. Nothing can stop you now. You are almost there and can't believe it! The wet soil is now knee deep. You are about a hundred yards from your destiny. You can now distinguish gold decorations at the top of the temple that must be worth millions. The wet soil is just below your waist. This is the best thing that has ever happened to you. No one will believe you. You are covered up to your elbows. Fifty more yards and everything will be yours. Up to your neck. Few more feet and everything will be great. You are the best adventurer in the whole world. Gulp.

Debt is the most patient and withy predator. It will first make you believe that it is weak and poses no threat. It will offer itself as food so you won't feel hungry. It will give you a hand so you think you can trust it. It will kneel before you as a servant so you think you can control it. You'll be so surprised when something goes wrong and you won't believe it's your fault. You will blame everyone and everything else. Maybe you made a bad choice in buying that certain something. Maybe you should've bought something else instead of that. You will embrace it so much that when you find yourself a goner, you will still believe that debt is your only friend. That debt is your only ticket out. You are so wrong.

Not knowing where you are or where you're going does not justify the outcome. It may be one of the causes, but you can't use it as an excuse. It is your fault if you don't make periodic checks to see that everything is good and going.

Don't let the water go all the way up to your neck to realize that something is wrong. Learn to see the tendencies, and make the right changes when it's merely ankle deep. What are the right changes? It could be an adjustment in the expenditures.

Scenario: You are laid off your work. You have 15,000 USD in your bank account. You used to earn 5,500 USD a month, and you are offered an underpaid 4,000 USD job. Your monthly expenditures are 5,000 USD. You have to decide to accept the job or to let it pass. What would you do?

- Case 1: You decide to let the job pass. Without getting into debt, you have 3 months to find a better job. A job that pays you the money you deserve to be paid for what you do.
- Case 2: You accept the job. Without lowering your expenditures or getting into debt, you will have 15 months to get a better job or to readjust your expenditures.

Scenario 2: You want to give your four children the best education there is (and besides, everyone in your family is sending their children to a private, renowned school). You currently earn: 11,000 USD a month. You have the following school options: Private Renowned (1,500 USD monthly), Private Normal (1,000 USD monthly) or Public (500 USD with extracurricular). Your current expenses without counting school tuition is 6,000 USD.

- Case 1: You enroll your children to the private renowned. They will attend school with their cousins. You have a deficit of 1,000 USD monthly. You will go in debt.
- Case 2: You enroll your children to a normal private school. They will not attend to a same level of education school as their cousins. You save 1,000 USD monthly.
- Case 3: You enroll your children to a public school and save 3,000 USD monthly.

Scenario 3: You have enough money to buy yourself a new car! You have worked your hat off and you have never given yourself a little treat. You have 50,000 USD in your bank account and spending it will not impact your sustainability. You can: Buy a High Class Car (80,000 USD with 4% interest rate), buy a Moderate Class Car (50,000 USD) or a Nice Used Car (30,000USD). You are going to buy it, you are not giving yourself the other option.

- Case 1: You buy the High Class Car and you are envied by everyone you know. You will end up paying the car in four years without a problem.
- Case 2: You buy the Moderate Class Car and don't go in debt.

- Case 3: You save 20,000 USD in your bank account and buy the third option.

What are the right choices? There are no right or wrong choices. Each choice you make will have a different outcome, and you must choose which outcome you wish to have. None of these scenarios (save maybe the first one) seem to be life threatening, but they could be.

In the first scenario, you're risking your sustainability to have a better outcome. In the second scenario, you're risking going in debt / saving money for the education of your children. In the third and last scenario, you're risking the amount of savings in your lake and/or your future Savings Lake growth for your personal wellbeing.

Going into debt means you will start feeding from your Savings Lake, which would in consequence decrease its size.

For example: You choose the first option from the second scenario. You will go into debt to give your children the best education you can find. We will assume you pay the whole tuition on a yearly basis at the end.

Year	Debt	Interests (4% rate)	Yearly Tuition Debt
1	0 USD	0 USD	12,000.00 USD
2	12,000.00 USD	480.00 USD	12,000.00 USD
3	24,480.00 USD	979.20 USD	12,000.00 USD
4	37,459.20 USD	1,498.37 USD	12,000.00 USD
5	50,957.57 USD	2,038.30 USD	12,000.00 USD
6	64,995.87 USD	2,599.83 USD	12,000.00 USD
7	79,595.71 USD	3,183.83 USD	12,000.00 USD

By the end of the year 7, you would owe the bank about 100,000 USD. If you had chosen the second option and invested it on something that gave you 4% annually, you would have the same amount, but in your bank account.

Chapter 13: Lifestyle level

This is the time of your life. You open your wallet and money is finally there. Your job paid off and you are on the receiving end of the cashier. You can hear the sound of it, and it's just wonderful. *Cha-ching.* You find yourself able to buy what you always wished for: a better house, a high class car, Dubai trips, fancy food, entertainment, watches (who doesn't like watches?), etc. You always considered yourself middle class, and it can all change now. You walk confident to your old car, and with an ear to ear smile you say, "So long, sucker."

When is it really time to change your lifestyle level? Those long term hard workers who have found themselves in this position often hesitate before spending their first deserved extra cash. They know that even hard earned money can go away easily, but they also believe that it's time to get a payback from all the effort.

There is no right answer as for the when, but there are answers that will prevent future growth. If you come from a middle class, your income will probably be similar to your expenditures. This new influx of money will mean that you will have a lot of spare. This is the time when you can use that extra cash to create ways to increase your income and diversify. Do you remember the example of the person who won the lottery and spent everything? His problem was that he had no water influx into his Savings Lake; it was all water going out. If you spend your new influx into no or low Savings Lake ratio items, you won't be prepared if things go south.

You must invest the extra cash so that the growth of that money pays for your change of lifestyle without you affecting the income from your current job/company. The interests of your savings will be paying for all those things you ever wished for, and your Savings Lake will continue growing with the current influx.

Example: This is your time to celebrate. Your income went from 125,000 USD to 400,000 USD in a year and it seems like it is going to sustain. Finally this is your moment; your American dream. What can you do now?

- Case 1: You change your house, change your car and go on a well-deserved trip. You increase your expenditures to just below 400,000 USD so you can still save. Your Savings Lake does go up with the increased income.
- Case 2: You invest your 275,000 USD without changing your current lifestyle. You expect that you will get a 10% above inflation growth with a

business you just created. At the end of the year you can use those 27,500 USD for yourself.

- Case 3: You save all of it into a low interest bank account investment. You might need the money at another time.

In the first case, your Savings Lake will increase, obviously, but your savings ratio will not increase. Your income got bigger and your expenditures did at the same rate. It would still be better than before, but you are not actually making wealthy choices.

In the second choice, you would increase your Savings Lake size by 275,000 USD per year and improve your lifestyle (as well as improving your savings ratio). I believe this is a win-win situation. You are prepared for the future, and your money is keeping its value. The good thing about this choice is that you will start seeing a correlation between your lifestyle with the amount of money you generate from your savings. You will strive to generate more money without really tapping into your Savings Lake.

The third choice is what I call a greedy point of view. Though your Savings Lake will obviously increase because you're not spending your income, you are not multiplying it. You don't want to share it with anyone or risk it. Since there is no risk, there is no growth. You will get nothing from this but a relief that the number in your bank account is increasing, though it's not increasing because it's growing, but because you're putting more money in it from your income. If your income goes sour, you'll start tapping into your Savings Lake and not into the interest of your savings.

What if I didn't find money in my wallet and my growth is pretty slim? How do I define my lifestyle level? If your lifestyle is causing you to get more debt, you are on the wrong level. If you don't see any growth on your Savings Lake, you could be on the wrong level (or you're not investing correctly). If your expenditures tend to be more of things that have a low savings ratio, and you're spending all your money, you're probably on the wrong level.

I know it's hard, not being on the level you were raised in (if you're newlywed or a new professional) at the beginning, but trying to start on a higher level means you will stay low for a while. If you earn 20 USD an hour, you can't expect to have a high class car. It is not because you don't deserve it, but because it will do you more harm than good.

Remember, using your savings growth (interests) to live is wiser than using your savings, but it is really about timing. You should not do this if you are on your early years: it will hinder your growth by far. You should seek to reinvest everything at the early years and pay yourself a little bit more on the latter without tapping into your Savings Lake growth.

Chapter 14: Companies

"Would you like a Coffee sir/ma'am?" your assistant asks you. You nod politely and she leaves the room. You look out the window of the twentieth floor at what you have accomplished. The company is by far better than what you believed at first. Who thought that selling marmalade would make so much money? You look far out to the outskirts of the city. You can see the huge reservoir you made with all your hard work. Still, how does it work? How do you factor this huge company (or small one) into your Savings Lake?

In reality, it's very simple. A company is an asset, just like a car, a house, or an investment in the stock market. Assets can change their value through time. A car generally decreases its value, a house generally increases its value similar to inflation, and a stock market investment varies depending to the current stock market. As a whole, the stock market is like a sine with a positive tendency. The big question would be how do you give your company a value?

You do it in the same way that you would give yourself a value. You add the real value of all your assets minus all your debt. Example: You own 50% of a service company. The accountant gives you the following balance sheet.

Your Company

Balance Sheet

December 31,2014

Assets

Current Assets

Cash	100,000	USD
Account receivable	50,000	USD
Inventory	0	USD
Total	**150,000**	**USD**

Property & Equip

Land	20,000	USD
Buildings	100,000	USD
Less: Accum. Dep	-20,000	USD
Total	**100,000**	**USD**
Total Assets	**250,000**	**USD**

Liabilities

Current liabilities

Accounts payable	30,000	USD
Salaries payable	10,000	USD
Taxes payable	5,000	USD
Total	45,000	USD

Long-term liabilities

Bank loan	30,000	USD
Total	30,000	USD

Total Liabilities **75,000** **USD**

Stockholders' equity

Capital Stock	100,000	USD
Retained earnings	75,000	USD

Total Stockholders' equity **175,000** **USD**

Total liabilities and equity **250,000** **USD**

You must consider the real value of your property and not the value in the balance sheet. You may have bought the land at 20,000 USD five years ago, but that piece of land could be worth 30,000 USD now. To calculate less earnings, the government lets you depreciate some of your assets such as buildings, cars, etc. You must ignore this and consider the real market value. In this scenario, your property is worth 150,000 USD (both construction and land).

In the current assets, you can see that your clients owe you 50,000 USD. You should not use this number in your company's value if this is an old or uncollectible debt. What should you consider old or uncollectible? Something that will be hard to collect in a short or medium term. I tend to be objective and prepare for the worst. If a client owes the company money and it has been three years since I performed the service, I consider it a loss. Yes, I will still do everything in my power to collect the debt, but I will not consider it earning until I get the money.

Cash	$	100,000.00
Clients	$	50,000.00
Building & Land	$	150,000.00
Liabilities	-$	75,000.00
	$	225,000.00
Equity		50%
Company Worth	$	112,500.00

Your company would be worth 112,500 USD in your Savings Lake. What would happen if the stockholders suddenly decided to cash out 20,000 USD each?

Your Savings Lake will increase 20,000 USD in your liquid money but decrease 20,000 USD in what your company is worth. Remember that cashing out may put your company in an unsustainable position. For example, if you and your partner decided to cash out 50,000 USD each, even if your company is really worth 225,000 USD, you would have to go in debt to keep operations going. In the end, you will lose future earnings by paying interests.

As a side note, a company can make the same mistakes as a person in their expenditures or investments. For example: a company has the chance to either buy the place where they're located, or rent it on a 5-year contract. They currently pay 20,000 USD monthly as rent (240,000 USD annually) or they could buy the place for 4,000,000 USD. They currently have enough money to pay it, but they have to decide to either invest the money in something else or buy. If they wait another 5 years to buy it with a 4.56% inflation per year, they would have to pay 5,000,000 USD. What should they do?

They are currently paying 6% of what the place is worth right now. By the end of the 5-year contract they would have paid 30% of its worth (1,200,000 USD). If they invested the 4,000,000 USD in a new line of production that lasts ten years, they would make 1,000,000 USD (earnings, not sale) a year. They expect a return of their money in four years (without inflation). The residue price of the production line after five years will be 2,000,000 USD.

Scenario 1 (buy it) after 5 years:

Company's Saving Lake = 5,000,000 USD (place is worth) + Other Earnings + Previous Assets

Scenario 2 (rent it) after 5 years:

Company's Saving Lake = 5,000,000 USD (Cash) – 1,200,000 USD (Rent) + 2,000,000 USD (Production Line)

Company's Saving Lake = 5,800,000 USD + Other Earnings + Previous Assets

Control Scenario after 5 years (you do nothing with the money):

Company's Saving Lake = 4,000,000 USD (cash) – 1,200,000 USD (Rent) + Other Earnings + Previous Assets

Company's Saving Lake = 2,800,000 USD + Other Earnings + Previous Assets

No matter what you choose, neither of the two examples is wrong. In the first scenario, aside from making your money keep its value through time, it also eliminates the rent. Therefore, you are actually making money (or at least avoiding spending it). In the second scenario, you are clearly making more money. You could now buy the place and have an extra 800,000 USD in cash. In the control scenario, you are losing money. You are losing 44% of what you could have if you do not buy the place or lose 52% if you don't invest the money in the production line.

It is very easy to get lost in the status quo and believe that by doing nothing you will not worsen the outcome. Yes, the money in your bank account is increasing because the income is constant, and you're spending less than what you are receiving as a person or a company, but you need to realize that you're not gaining any profit for what you've already saved. You are losing opportunity.

Chapter 15: Conclusion

You just graduated from university in marketing. A wonderful life back home awaits you. You don't know how much people earn at your age in your hometown, so you go out asking before getting your first job. You go well dressed, have a good interview and you land a job at a local supermarket. Since you still live with your family, your first paycheck goes directly into your bank account. You start taking note of everything you spend your money on.

> **Tip:** Without indicators, you will have a feeling of what you are doing, but you will not know for sure. Create your "dashboard" and start working with it. You will find several useful indicators in this book.

A year goes by and everything is working in your favor. You just received a bump in your salary of 5%. You are extremely happy, but when you go out to buy things, you notice that you could buy almost the same as a year before.

> **Tip:** Use the rule of the double: Know in how many years you need to have double in your Savings Lake so that you

have an equivalent acquisition power. Your goal must always be above that number. Below Inflation growth means you are losing money. Check the growth factor considering inflation.

$$Factor = \frac{(1 + \%\ Interest\ Rate\ offered)}{(1 + \%\ Inflation)}$$

Something might be wrong, yet when you look at your bank account, you noticed that you saved around 30% of what you made that previous year. Yet, the money just stayed there. You go to the bank and open an investment account that will give you 2% a year. Saving money is hard, you think.

You are 25 years old now and you see yourself with a house at the age of 35. You start adding up all your paychecks to that date and you notice that it is not what you expected. Maybe you are in the wrong job. You go check several other places, but they expect for you to have at least 3 years of experience for a better position.

Tip: Review yourself and compare your findings to your expectations. Do the math of how much you are earning (and how much you will most likely earn) and what you want for your future. If you know you are underachieving, then it means you can actually do something. Else, you are just going with the flow. Make a change before it matters.

You rethink your position and try to get the best out of your current situation. You start investigating ways to increase the supermarket's profitability. You also learn how to better position the products to increase sales. Everyone around you is just too used to their job that they see it like that: a job. You know this is an opportunity to learn how everything works.

Tip: Time is your ally. Invest your free time to increase your knowledge of something that might affect your expertise directly or indirectly. Someone who is a construction worker who knows accounting might have an easier time making a construction company than someone who does not. Well-used time might increase both the economical and knowledge gap between you and other people.

Your coworkers spend almost all their money on living and you are sure you don't want to be one of them. They might be nice people and you respect them, but you want something more. You decrease your expenditures without affecting your social life. You can still go out with your friends, but you manage the amount of money you spend at the places you go.

Tip: Your spending defines your savings percentage and your economical future. You will have a lifelong problem if your expenditures are equal or greater than your income. If you spend all your money in things with a savings ratio near zero, you will be poor or will have to overwork all your life.

$$Saving\ Lake\ Deposit\ Ratio = \frac{\sum(Expend * C) + (Income - \sum Expend)}{Income}$$

Remember, there are three things you can spend your money on: **Investment** (grows with time), Savings (maintains or slightly decreases its value through time) and **Void** (no remaining value).

Time goes by and you start noticing how your savings go up. Still, even after investing your money in that 2% interest rate bond you know that it is not going up fast enough. You also see that all your savings are in money and you consider buying assets. You look around and see that if you buy a car and resell it you can earn a lot more than what the bank gives you. If you do it in the same year, the car does not lose value.

Tip: The composition of the Savings Lake is made of liquid savings, assets and debt. Liquid savings is money you can use anytime you like. Generally, money by itself has little to no growth. If you buy a 30-day bond and you cannot use the money, it is an asset, not liquid savings.

$$Savings\ Lake = Liquid\ Savs\ (\$)$$
$$+ Captive\ Savs\ (Assets)$$
$$- Savings\ Oil\ (Debt)$$

Remember to keep records of your Savings Lake at different periods so you can see if you are actually growing or not.

$$Savings\ Grow\ Rate$$

$$= \frac{\frac{Savings\ Lake\ 2014}{(1 + Inflation\ between\ 2014\ and\ 2013)} - Savings\ Lake\ 2013}{Savings\ Lake\ 2013}$$

You have enough money to buy two cars at once and you do it. You see that you are earning money faster now. You continue to work hard in the supermarket and you implement what you learned on your spare time. The manager notices your effort and gives you a small bump again before the yearly increase. You know it is not much, but his noticing means you are doing it right.

Tip: Money multiplication is what makes a person wealthy. If you buy a house to rent, the house will take around 20 years to pay for itself (depends on the rent percentage of course). If after you get all your money back, you buy another house, it'll take half the time to buy a third one of equal value, then less to buy the fourth and so on. The longer you wait to cash out, the faster your money grows. If you are impatient and always cash out right away, you will never become wealthy.

You notice that in certain places in the country you can find low priced cars that go for much more in your city. You go to the bank and ask for a big loan. They deny it because you have no credit score. You get a credit card

102

with a low credit limit. You ask someone else from your family to be part of the business and you get enough money to buy a couple of cars. You see that by investing their money you have far more cars to sell and earn more money overall.

Tip: Investing debt is magic. You create growth out of someone else's pocket and keep it some for yourself. Yet, as powerful as it may be, it works equally against you. A wrong turn might leave you with an unpayable debt. The trick is to know how much you can handle.

If your income is 10,000 USD and your expenditure is 9,000 USD, you can use the extra 1,000 USD to go in debt and buy a car to resell. If for whatever reason you are unable to sell the car, you still have those extra 1,000 USD to pay to the bank each month.

You grow close to one of your old friends, and decide to marry her. You convince her not to overspend their savings in the wedding, and she agrees. Both believe that a moderate present means a better future. You decide not to have kids until some time has passed.

> **Tip:** Your life decisions affect your economical outcome. If you decide to have kids, you will have to pay their living expenses. By knowing the consequences of your actions before doing anything, you will be able to plan accordingly. Perhaps it is better to wait a couple of years before taking that first step. Future growth is affecting by today's decision. Make informed decisions.

She is a bit desperate in forcing the two of you to make the decision of buying a house. You disagree and convince her that buying a house at that moment would prevent future growth and that you are making far more money in your current business.

You try to avoid having many liquid savings (cash in the bank) because they offer low growth and focus on buying fast return assets with a moderate grow. You know that it does not matter if you earn 7% with each car sell as long as you can repeat the operation several times in a year.

> **Tip:** Having all your money in the bank without making any real investment means that you will lose money each year due to inflation, and that your Savings Lake is not really working. You need to focus on having assets that

> will make your Savings Lake grow by its own. Debt will increase either your liquid savings or your assets, but it will also prevent future growth if the interest rate paid is greater than the growth of the asset.

You check your credit score again and you are now capable or asking for a business loan. You increase the number of cars you buy and sell. You change your job at the supermarket and go with an entrepreneur who wants to open a business. He offers you a similar payment to the one you received at your previous job and a bit of equity. You cannot believe it, but you notice that the same mistakes that the people at the supermarket made are the same mistakes other people make at different businesses, even if it is in a completely different field. You use what you learned at how to manage a supermarket and implement it at your new job.

> **Tip:** You need a credit score if you want to use debt to grow. Keep a credit card and use it just as if you were using cash. Do not increase your expenditures. Do not go into debt. Pay immediately what you buy.

You decide to have a child with your wife. You know this will not make you richer economically, but it is the right step to take. You have everything covered. You took your time to make this change and it will have no negative effects in your life. Hard decisions with the right planning mean no negative impacts.

> **Tip:** Good planning and careful execution means a high probability of a great outcome. Obviously, bad things can happen, but at least they were not self-imposed. If you go far overboard on your expenses, you will for sure have an economical problem. These are self-imposed problems.

Everything is just going perfect. Yes, perhaps you did not expect to have two kids instead of just one, but you are far better prepared than most people you know. There is a big difference from life just happening to giving a direction to your life. Remember that you are as ignorant to everything as you want to be.

> **Tip:** If you don't know something, investigate on the internet. If you do not find the answer, ask others. If none of the answers are good enough for you, study and then create the path for others. Ignorance is not bliss, because the outcome will not be the same.

Your company is working great and you are indeed growing. You keep on studying to keep yourself up to date. You work hard and keep striving for your goals. Somehow, you find yourself earning more than what you actually need. You decide not to get flustered with the amount of money you are receiving and you take a conservative position in your expenditures. Yes, you have enough money to buy a bigger house, a better car, a better school, and a better vacation, but you still believe you can go further. You increase your lifestyle but just by a nudge, enough for you to feel better, but conservatively enough that you can grow extremely fast.

> **Tip:** Maintain your lifestyle so that you don't eat your savings. Your lifestyle expenditures should not affect your Savings Lake grow. If your income doubles, do not double your expenditures.

You have several companies and you manage, each one independent from one another. You check your Savings Lake size every three months to know your direction. Indirectly, by checking your Savings Lake you are checking each of your companies. Remember that even though companies are assets in your Savings Lake, people still work in them. Be mindful that if you help people grow (in a healthy way), they will in return make your company grow.

> **Tip:** Help your company grow healthy with the help of the people who work there. If you make them sink, you will sincerely get nowhere.

Epilogue

You yawn as you wake up from a deep slumber. You open your eyes and see that the lake you believed you had is nothing more than a small pond. You do not panic, as you know that you have no real control of what already is, but you do have control of what will be. Perhaps you will not win the lottery; perhaps you will not have skyscrapers with your name, but someday the small pond in front of you will grow bigger. Someday your pond will turn into a lake. It is just a matter of time, and hard work.

www.ingramcontent.com/pod-product-compliance
Lightning Source LLC
Chambersburg PA
CBHW070906180526
45168CB00005B/1944